How To Make Mor

Presented to

_____

On _____

By _____

How to Make Money on eBay

Without Using Any of Your own Money
A 24-Hour Success Guide: Start Earning
Cash within 24 Hours   Guaranteed!

DAN GIBSON

© 2012 Kajoku Publishing. All rights reserved.
Printed in the United Kingdom.

Copyright notice
No part of this publication may be reproduced or transmitted in any form or by any means, mechanical or electronic, including photocopying and recording, or by any information storage and retrieval system, without permission in writing from author or publisher.

ISBN: 978-0-954999-3-77

How to make money on eBay &is no way authorised by, endorsed, or affiliated with eBay or its subsidiaries. All references to eBay and other trade marked properties are used in accordance with the Fair Use Doctrine and are not meant for advertising or other commercial purposes.

Books published by Kajoku Publishing are available at special quantity discounts to use as premiums and sales promotions, or for use in corporate training programs. For more information, please write to Kajoku Publishing, Kajoku House, PO Box 274, Kent DA7 9AG, email sales@kajoku.com, call 07956 515 868 or contact your local bookstore.

Disclaimer Notice
The publisher (Kajoku Publishing) accepts no liability whatsoever for any consequence of transactions entered into. There is risk in all business activity. Future profits are neither guaranteed nor implied. Any persons entering into any business arrangement should seek professional advice, especially before entering any binding agreements. The publisher reserves the right to terminate partnership agreements for breaches of rules of said agreement or knowingly bringing the name of Kajoku Publishing into disrepute.
Neither previous advertising materials nor text of this publication shall constitute any terms of said agreements.
The publisher will not be liable for any expenses incurred by the participant in active Associate participation with Kajoku Publishing.

How To Make Money On eBay

Acknowledgements

I would like to thank my Lord and Saviour Jesus Christ who through him all things are possible.

I d like to thank my lovely wife and business partner Tanya. Thank you darling for putting up with all those late nights and looking after the children while this book was written.

I d like to thank my father Lee, my mother Pauline, who both never fail to inspire me whatever difficulties I may come across, they ve taught me, patience, persistence and perseverance.

I d like to thank my numerous friends, family and colleagues, you know who you are. Thank you for all your support and encouragement, and thanks for believing in me.

I d like to thank you the reader for taking the first positive steps to creating multiple streams of eBay income.

Dan Gibson
How to Make Money on eBay

CONTENTS PAGE

INTRODUCTION 7

CHAPTER 1
How To Unlock The Hidden Cash Potential Of Your Unwanted Items 12

CHAPTER 2
Discover The Secrets Of Items That Are Guaranteed To Sell 20

CHAPTER 3
How To Profit From Sales You Don t Have To Make 27

CHAPTER 4
Learn How To Develop And Sell Your Ideas 35

CHAPTER 5
Discover The Secrets Of How To Sell At The Highest Price 44

CHAPTER 6
How To Successfully Market And Sell 48

CHAPTER 7
How To Make Money Without Selling Anything 54

CHAPTER 8
How To Unleash The Ebay Money Making Machine
66

CHAPTER 9
How To Make Money In Auto-pilot 76

CHAPTER 10
How To Get All The Customers You Need With Web Traffic Secrets 85

BONUS CHAPTER
How To Make Money Blogging 94

My Make Money on eBay Notes 108

My Make Money on eBay Action Plan 115

INTRODUCTION

Introduction

Welcome to How to Make Money on eBay Without Using Any of Your Own Money... In this book I will share with you 10 ways of making a decent living on eBay with little or no capital outlay whatsoever.

What is eBay?

EBay is a website; it s a place to; buy, sell, shop and collect. EBay is free for buyers and inexpensive for sellers to use. EBay s UK store can be found by entering www.ebay.co.uk into any web browser.

Since eBay's founding in 1995 it has become the world's largest online marketplace. It has a community of millions of individuals, small businesses, and big businesses worldwide who buy and sell millions of items of every kind imaginable on a daily basis. Prices range from one penny to hundreds of thousands or even millions of pounds.

To read more background information on eBay go to http://pages.ebay.com/aboutebay/thecompany/companyoverview.html

Introduction

EBay is currently the UK s largest online marketplace. It has over 14 million active users and has several thousand people relying on it for their income. I believe that you too can make a decent living on eBay by working smartly and consistently.

How to use this book.

In this book How to make money on eBay without spending any money & I will show you ten ways of making a reasonable amount of money without spending your own money. As you complete each chapter I recommend that you implement what you ve learnt as soon as possible so you can start earning money.

How this book is organised

This book is divided into three parts.

Part 1 Will show you how to sell products on eBay.

Part 2 Will show you how to use eBay to make money without physically selling any products.

Part 3 Will show you how to market your products and services.

Introduction

At the back of this book you will find a section entitled My Make Money on eBay Notes , I suggest that you use this section to make notes as you read this book so you can refer to them later. The section entitled My Make Money on eBay Action will help you to devise a structured action plan to aid your money making endeavours.

My blog website

In most of the chapters I refer to my Blog site http://ebayforprofit.blogspot.com where you ll find up-to-date information and resources to help you.

Who this book is aimed at

If you are completely new to eBay this book will help you make all the right moves the first time round, taking a lot of the guess work out of selling on eBay. If you re a seasoned eBayer then you ll find a lot of useful tips in this book particularly in the latter chapters. Unless you re already an eBay Millionaire then I m pretty sure you ll find this book useful.

Introduction

If you carefully follow all or even some of these approaches, I assure you that you will make money. So I wish you all the best in this endeavour, and I hope you enjoy reading this book as much as I have enjoyed writing it.

CHAPTER 1

How To Unlock The Hidden Cash Potential Of Your Unwanted Items

Unlock Hidden Cash Potential

What is a traditional home clearout sale?

A traditional home clearout sale typically happens in your front yard, where you put out tables on a particular day when the weather is at its best and arrange all your household items that you no longer need with price tags and put them up for sale. You create flyers and post them all around the neighbourhood to publicise your home clearout sale, and hope to see hordes of people at the sale event. People come by, browse through the items you have put up for sale, pick out what they like, check the price tag, and buy it. At the end of a good day, you end up selling everything and counting your earnings. You re happy because you met your targets, and you got rid of all those things that you no longer need for cash. And your total monetary investment has been zero.

Home clearout sale on eBay.

You can do the same on eBay but it will be better than a home clearout sale   as it will be a home clearout sale auction. More people will come to your eBay home clearout

Unlock Hidden Cash Potential

sale auction and your items will be sold to the highest bidder rather than the thrift shopper that has haggled down the price.

How to set up a home clearout sale on eBay.

Here s a step by step description of how to set up a home clearout sale on eBay:

Step 1: Gather the items you want to sell from around your house, check your loft, wardrobe, and shed, the more items the better.

Step 2: Choose a date to hold the sale. Currently eBay allows you to list your items for 1, 3, 5, 7 or 10 days. The final day of your home clearout sale is by far the most important. Potential buyers will come and browse through your items but may bid in the last moments of the sale. Therefore make sure your listings don t end on days or at times where people are less likely to be at their computers such as; public holidays and weekends or during rush hour for example.

Unlock Hidden Cash Potential

Step 3: Move all of your home clearout items into one place, such as the garage or a storage area, so you can access them easily.

Step 4: Determine your final price for everything and take a photograph of each item. You ll use the photos later when you post the items on eBay.

Step 5: Do a little market research: browse through the item category and look at similar items from other eBay sellers. Compare it with your product and see if your product justifies the price that you are asking. Lower or raise your item s price appropriately. This step will also help you judge how the market is doing in this category.

For example, if there are a lot of similar items in this category, then there will be tough competition for your product and you might have to lower your item s price further. In some cases, you might even have to sell your item at a price lower than its original purchase price, but this

Unlock Hidden Cash Potential

should not bother you, after all these items have been gathering dust in the loft for ages.

Step 6: Write a brief but complete description of the product. For example, if it is an electronic item, be sure to include all the relevant technical specifications and dimensions for it. Put in your description everything you can that relates to the item. Include the photo you took in your description, remember buyers can t physically feel or see the product, they are relying on your, photos and descriptive words to help them decide whether they are to purchase your item or not. It is always a good idea to be honest in your descriptions too, for example if your item has a little scratch or is damaged, mention it, (honesty is the best policy).

For example, you can say it has a superficial scratch on the left hand side, but this does not by any means affect the performance of the item.

Another thing you can add to improve your chances is an offer to answer any questions that potential buyers may have.

Unlock Hidden Cash Potential

I have done this many times in the past with a huge success rate. There is also an option to publish your questions and answers for other customers to read.

Step 7: Post each and every item in the appropriate eBay category, along with the photo, description and the starting bid.

Step 8: Look around on the Internet for some user reviews and ratings for the item you are selling. You ll find plenty of ratings and reviews on the Internet for almost all the items that you are selling, simply type review for x product (replacing the x for the product name of your item) into a search engine of your choice.

Copy and paste the user review and/or rating and add that to your product description on eBay. Adding a review or rating to your product most definitely increases your chances of selling it.

Unlock Hidden Cash Potential

Step 9: Once you have placed all your items for sale in the appropriate eBay category, with the right prices, pictures and descriptions, take a quick glance at all of them to make sure everything is in place and that everything looks attractive to a prospective buyer. If it doesn t, go back and start over from step 1. If everything is okay, you re good to go.

Step 10: Sit back and relax and let buyers visit your eBay home clearout sale. Be sure to keep an eye on your email in case you have received questions from prospective buyers. I suggest that you answer questions as quickly as possible, to engage your buyer in dialogue. When a buyer is interested in your item and proposes to buy it, an eBay notification will be sent to your email address and you can move forward and complete the transaction.

Step 11: At the end of the sale, see what you ve sold and count your earnings. If you didn t make as much money as you expected, don t be discouraged. As your eBay selling experience increases so will your earnings. So if you re not able to sell all your items the first time round, re-list them. Don t take your items off the eBay shelf. There is still a chance that you ll find a buyer the next time round. Put aside some of your profit to re-invest into other eBay money making ventures described within this book.

Further help
To get help and tips with setting up a new, eBay account for free go to my blog website;

http://ebayforprofit.blogspot.com

CHAPTER 2

Discover The Secrets Of Items That Are Guaranteed To Sell

Items Guaranteed To Sell

I m going to share with you in this chapter some very valuable tips and tricks that you ll be able to use whether you have been selling on eBay for a while, are a new eBay seller, or are thinking about selling on eBay. I m about to show you a hidden secret on eBay where you can find niche, hot items that are guaranteed to sell!

Go directly to http://pages.ebay.co.uk/wantitnow/, many people use this section to place requests for items that they actually want to buy. Sellers may have heard of this section but tend not to use it to its full potential because of their lack of knowledge. It s the Want It Now section (see fig.1 below).

Items Guaranteed To Sell

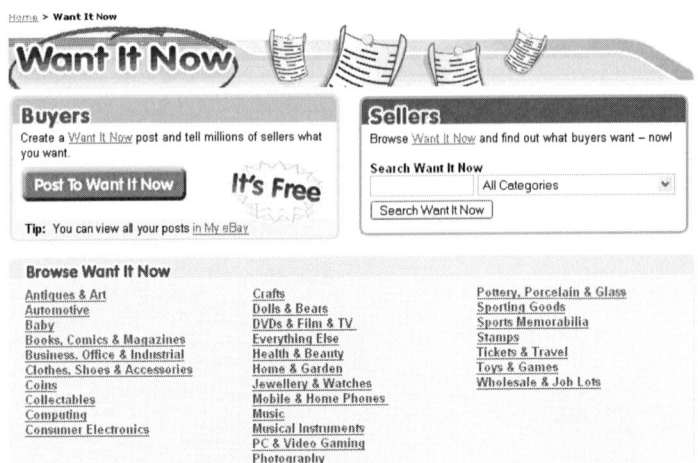

Fig. 1

What is the "Want It Now Section" section?

The Want It Now section is truly amazing for gathering niche hot items. Unfortunately a lot of people don t know how to use it to implement it into their eBay business. This section is basically a collection of posts that shoppers put up that are requesting items that they want to buy, items that they weren t able to find on the main auction section on eBay.

Items Guaranteed To Sell

What the "Want It Now Section" section can be used for.

The basic idea is to grab hold of a niche item that a customer desperately wants from this section, and find it in your home or neighbourhood store and sell it to the customer. Since this is a niche hot item and the customer Wants It Now , you can even charge a higher premium for it, gaining up to 300% profit on the sale.

How the "Want It Now Section" section can be used

Let me show you how to use the Want It Now Section section using a step-by-step approach.

Let s go to the books category of the Want It Now section, you will notice that there are numerous books required by buyers who have money in their pockets ready to give to you because these are the items that they want you to sell them NOW, items that they urgently need.

If you look carefully at fig. 2, you can see 327 hot niche items in the books category of the Want It Now section (you can also look through the different book categories on

Items Guaranteed To Sell

the left hand side under Narrow Your Results). This means that there are 327 hot and rare books that people want NOW and will pay a reasonable price to get them. Now that s a big opportunity for any eBay seller right there.

327 Want It Now posts found in Books, Comics
Post Title
The Hunter is Death by T V Bulpin
A book with photographs of dessert/nature scenes
Singer model 457 stylist Zig Zag SERVICE MANUAL.
1980s copies of Security Installer Magazine
K203 - Working for Health!
Egmont Books Thomas Tank Engine 56 - 60
From Monk to Busman by Bertram Cannell
Michelangelo Opera completa Taschen

Fig. 2

How to benefit from the "Want It Now" Section

If we were to take all of this information, the 327 posts, look through all the web pages (not necessarily every single post) and look for trends repeating keywords, product names that repeat, particular styles of products, items that have been

Items Guaranteed To Sell

requested from numerous shoppers — this itself would create a hot niche market for you and you can pretty much guarantee that the item would sell. What you can do is actually inform these shoppers that you have the niche item that they re looking for and redirect them to your eBay page.

The advantages of this strategy:
- Not only is this a hot item, it takes away the guesswork of what to sell on eBay. And with the ever-increasing eBay fees, having items that sell the first time you put them on eBay will keep your fees lower and your profits higher.

There are a number of software tools that can help you conduct trend analysis. Trends such as searches made by potential buyers for items that they did not find (taking the guess work out of what people are looking for).

AuctionYen (see Fig. 3 below) is designed specifically for eBay, it can show you all the trends that you re looking for in a few clicks.

Items Guaranteed To Sell

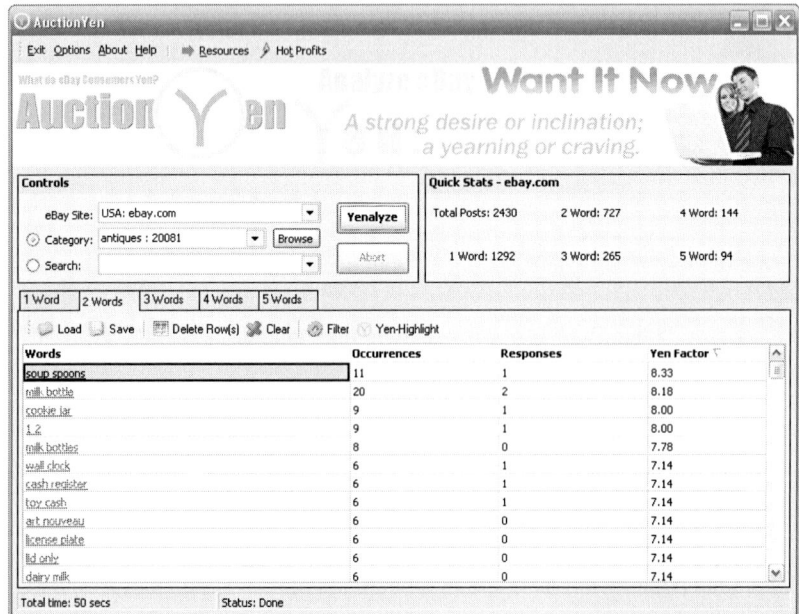

Fig. 3

Once you ve decided on your niche items you simply have to source them and list them just as you listed for your home clearout sale.

Further help

To get help and tips with setting up a new AuctionYen account go to my blog website;

http://ebayforprofit.blogspot.com

CHAPTER 3

How To Profit From Sales You Don t Have To Make

Profit From Sales You Don t Have To Make

What is drop-shipping?

Drop-shipping is another way to make money online on sites like eBay. Drop shipping can be described as a supply chain management technique in which the retailer does not keep goods in stock, but instead transfers customer orders and shipment details to either the manufacturer or a wholesaler, who then ships the goods directly to the customer . Effectively you are the retailer and you make your profit on the difference between the wholesale and retail price. If you use a drop-shipper, there is no need to physically send the product it is all done for you after you ve sold the item for a profit and sent the order details to the drop-shipper.

How does drop-shipping work?

Before I show you how to implement this strategy step-by-step, let me explain to you by means of a diagram how it works.

Profit From Sales You Don t Have To Make

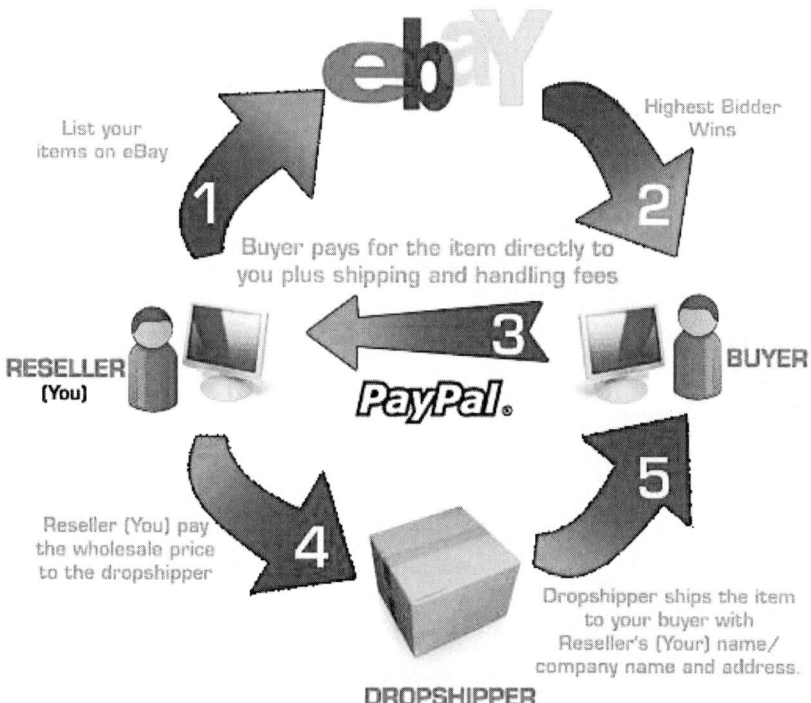

Fig. 4

From Fig. 4 above we can see that there are 5 processes, namely;

1. List your items - it s a good idea to choose products that you like or are familiar with. The chapter Discover The Secrets Of Items That Are Guaranteed To Sell will help you choose a product.

Profit From Sales You Don t Have To Make

2. List your product on eBay. The chapter How To Unlock The Hidden Cash Potential Of Your Unwanted Items will explain the steps to do this.
3. Sell your products - allow someone to purchase and pay via Paypal, or by cheque or cash.
4. Once you ve confirmed receipt of the payment you can confidently place the order with the supplier.
5. The supplier dispatches the products to your customer directly, under your agreed instructions.

The following is a typical example: A drop-shipping company has a new top of the range digital camera for £89 in stock. You sell the camcorder for the best price you can above the drop-shippers price and once the auction or sale is complete, you pay the drop-shipper the £89 and email them the buyers name and address; they then post the digital camera for you leaving you to take the profit.

Profit From Sales You Don t Have To Make

How to find a drop-shipping company

To find a drop-shipping company simply type eBay drop-shippers or drop-shippers into your favourite search engine to get a list of drop-shippers. Once you get the search results list simply do your research to find suitable drop-shippers for your chosen product niche.

What to be weary of when dealing with drop-shippers
Once you ve contacted them, be sure to read their terms and conditions and find out their delivery timeframes. This is important, as you don t want your customers waiting around for their products to arrive. Other things to consider would be; turnaround times (time taken for the products to get to your customer), returns policies for faulty or unwanted goods, and what type of delivery tracking systems they have in place, which will be handy in cases where the customers delivery may have gone astray.

It would be in your best interest to compare their product prices with those within the completed items list on eBay to

Profit From Sales You Don t Have To Make

ensure that your products are competitively priced. For more on the completed items list see the chapter entitled Discover The Secrets Of Items That Are Guaranteed To Sell .

The Benefits of drop-shipping

Drop-shipping is a convenient way to sell things on eBay without having to stock the items yourself. Drop-shipping ca offer you a high profit margin and the method makes it easier for you to sell products because you don t have to handle any shipping yourself. Drop-shipping allows you to buy the item from your drop-shipper when you ve got a confirmed order from your eBay customer. Once you ve provided your drop-shipper with your customers order details you can then simply move onto the next customer s order.

The table in Fig. 5 provides you with some of the pros and cons of using the drop-shipping technique.

Profit From Sales You Don t Have To Make

PROS	CONS
No need for a warehouse	No control over the shipping process including time to get there
No need to handle products	No control control over your inventory
Allows anyone to be able to sell anything without needing the above	
No need to have a lot of money to start	
No need to deal with physically shipping the product	
No need to buy the product until after it has sold	
No need to have to create shipping labels	
No need to replace product returns	

Fig. 5

In my opinion, one of the biggest problems that you could encounter is the possibility of the drop-shipper going out of business as this may leave you with outstanding orders to fill. This is a rarity, but never the less a reality. It s therefore always best practice to vet your drop-shippers, do your home work, get references, speak to existing clients that they may have used their services, check how long they have been trading, have a look at their accounts, for example using government websites like www.companieshouse.gov.uk.

Profit From Sales You Don t Have To Make

Further help

For details and links to drop-shippers visit my blog website:

http://ebayforprofit.blogspot.com

CHAPTER 4

Learn How To Develop And Sell Your Ideas

How To Develop And Sell Your Ideas

If you want to make money on eBay without spending any money, think of an idea that no one has thought of before and market it on eBay. You are going to think of something that would be nice if it existed, and make it a reality.

To sell your idea on eBay, you have to be creative and think out-of-the-box . I have known people who have come up with unique ideas and made huge amounts of money on eBay without spending a penny. I will show you a step-by-step approach of how to come up with a unique business idea that will set you apart from the rest of the eBay sellers and fetch you huge profit margins.

Products With Limitations

Have you ever used something and wished it could do a little bit more? Many great products fall into this category; an example is a well known lightweight toddler s push chair. It s great for airplane travel, but problematic when used on a trip to the local shopping centre. Shopping bags cannot be loaded onto the handles as the weight of the shopping can

How To Develop And Sell Your Ideas

make the push chair topple over. Not great for a busy mum attempting to do a weeks worth of grocery shopping! One mum who had enough of her toppling push chair designed a shopping bag that actually attaches underneath the push chair therefore creating a safe way of carrying shopping home without the risk of the push chair toppling. This item is currently for sale exclusively on eBay! Are there any every day items you use that are great but you wish could do just a little bit more? How many times have you said wouldn t be great if &? If you ve said it, the chances are there are tens, hundreds, maybe even thousands of people out there who have said the exact same words but done nothing about it. Those words could be your next eBay money-making idea!

Something You Love
We all have our favourite pastimes. Things we do in our spare time, things we enjoy doing, or perhaps things that we re good at. If there is something you are passionate about you could somehow make a product out of it and sell it on

How To Develop And Sell Your Ideas

eBay. A friend of mine is a very experienced laptop computer engineer. For several years he has run a successful computer business and has accumulated knowledge about pretty much everything there is to know about laptop computers. Times have since changed and he now sells his knowledge on eBay. How? In the form of a book. This book contains a step-by-step instruction guide of how to fix a broken laptop screen. The book can save the reader hundreds of pounds at a fraction of the cost. What are you good at? What are you passionate about? Whether its personalised T-shirts or a book about your area of interest, the chances are there are many people out there who want what you have to offer.

Something You Hate
You don t have to look far to find something that just ruins the flow of your day. What was the last project you did that really irked you? Perhaps there s an awkward workaround that you find yourself repeating time and time again and you

How To Develop And Sell Your Ideas

just wish you had a neat solution. Maybe that solution is your next product idea!

Let's Get Creative!

Now it s time for you to get your creative juices flowing. To do this you need to set aside 15 minutes and grab a pen and a stopwatch (or any device with an alarm eg mobile phone). You are about to think of your very own idea. Use the My Make Money on eBay Notes section at the back of this book to write on.

Warm-up Exercise

To get the creative side of your brain working I would like you to set your stopwatch for 1 minute and in that time write down 10 uses for a paperclip. Repeat the exercise, but this time you have 2 minutes to write down 25 uses (that s 15 more). Now the final time you have 3 minutes to write down 40 uses for a paper clip. Some example uses are: earrings, necklace, key, and of course, a paper clip!

How To Develop And Sell Your Ideas

How many did you get? Well done if you found 40. Great effort for 25 or more. If you found 10 to 25 that s good too. No matter how many uses you found the key here is to stretch you brain and to practice thinking outside the box. You can repeat this exercise anytime you want to simply substituting the paper clip for anything else. Some examples are a ruler, a leaf, an apple, a water bottle, and a pen to name a few.

Brainstorming Exercise 1: A Few of Your Favourite Things
Use 3 minutes to write down all the things you love doing or experiencing, or are passionate about. Your list should have at least 10 items.

Next use 5 minutes to write down 3 ways that each item can be useful to someone else. For example if you wrote growing flowers, you may write tips on how to grow a perfect flower bed or tell someone what my best gardening tools are .

How To Develop And Sell Your Ideas

Finally look at your second list and write down how the items can be developed into a product or service. For example top gardening tips book or grow your own perfect flower bed kit .

Brainstorming Exercise 2: Pet Hates
Use 3 minutes to write down all the things you hate doing or experiencing. Include any awkward work-arounds you find yourself doing. Go through a typical day or event for inspiration. Your list should have at least 10 items.

Next use 5 minutes to write down 3 ways that you can avoid or solve or make that pet hate go away. For example if you wrote losing all my contacts on my sim card when my phone gets lost , you may write somehow keeping a copy of my phonebook safe . Finally look at your second list and write down how the items can be developed into a product or service. For example phone contact back-up gadget .

How To Develop And Sell Your Ideas

The Beauty of eBay

The beauty of using eBay is that firstly, you can test your idea out very quickly and inexpensively. Unlike all the rigmarole you would have to go through to get your product on the shelf of any chain supermarket, you can make a few, sell them, and take it from there. Secondly, you can conduct your market research as you go along. The number of purchases of your product and the number of page views will give you a good indicator of the demand for your product. You can test out different price points to see what amount the punters are willing to pay. A friend of mine listed a home-made product for sale at a buy-it-now price of £1.99. no one bought it. He then listed the item at £10.95 and it sold out! Sometimes people are not always looking for the cheapest item. Too cheap can be a bad thing. It s all down to the buyer s perception of value for money. And finally eBay is just the beginning! Once you ve fine tuned your product you could try selling it through other outlets. And if your success continues, you could make a commercial-grade product and

How To Develop And Sell Your Ideas

approach retailers with it as a viable product for their shelves. Who knows where your idea will take you!

With the tips I ve taught you in this chapter, you too can think of your own innovative ideas. Inspiration can come from anywhere and it can take your product to eBay and beyond. I challenge you today to look at the problems and passions in your life through fresh and creative eyes. What problems can you solve today? You never know which idea is going to be the next eBay best seller.

CHAPTER 5

Discover The Secrets Of How To Sell At The Highest Price

How To Sell At The Highest Price

The completed listings section on eBay is one of the most powerful untapped features on the eBay website. You can use this section to pre-determine what an item could sell for and better still you can find the best way to maximise your selling price, allowing you to get the highest selling prices possible.

Allow me to explain by taking you through the steps.

Step 1 - Let s say you wanted to sell a Wii fit. Enter wii fit and select the completed listings only link. (NB: at that point you will be directed to log into your eBay account to proceed)

Step 2 Enter wii fit in the search box.

How To Sell At The Highest Price

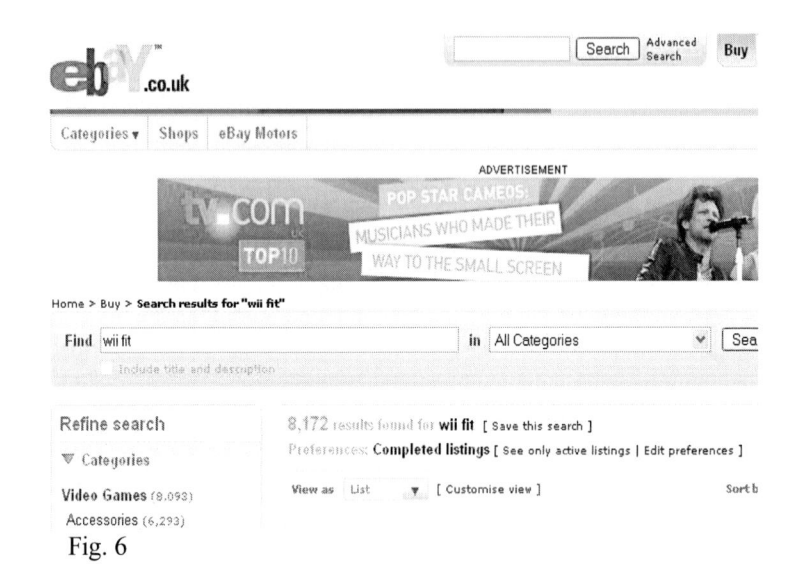

Fig. 6

Step 3 - Select in the sort by section **Price: highest first**, as we want to make as much money as possible by selling at the highest price possible.

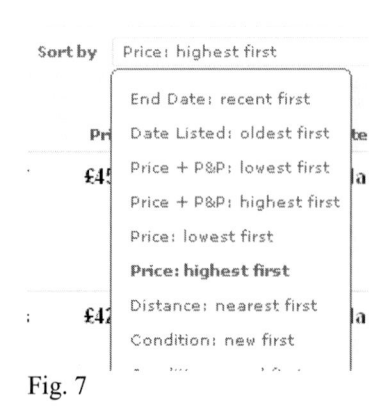

Fig. 7

Step 4 - Scroll through the completed listings as I have done

How To Sell At The Highest Price

in the example making a note of the actual prices that the wii fit sold for. In this example it was sold between £367.99 and £380.

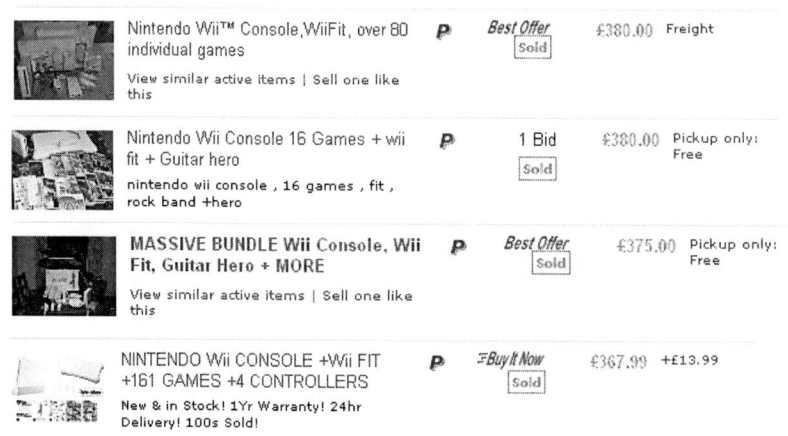

	Nintendo Wii™ Console,WiiFit, over 80 individual games View similar active items | Sell one like this	P	Best Offer Sold	£380.00	Freight
	Nintendo Wii Console 16 Games + wii fit + Guitar hero nintendo wii console , 16 games , fit , rock band +hero	P	1 Bid Sold	£380.00	Pickup only: Free
	MASSIVE BUNDLE Wii Console, Wii Fit, Guitar Hero + MORE View similar active items | Sell one like this	P	Best Offer Sold	£375.00	Pickup only: Free
	NINTENDO Wii CONSOLE +Wii FIT +161 GAMES +4 CONTROLLERS New & in Stock! 1Yr Warranty! 24hr Delivery! 100s Sold!	P	=Buy It Now Sold	£367.99	+£13.99

Fig. 8

(This means that you can actual realistically achieve this selling price if you have idental items.)

Step 5 - Go through each of the completed listings and study the contents for each. Provide the same contents and you re a winner! If its more games needed then try and source them, if its reviews, then also find them. Your aim is to maximise your selling price, hence maximising your profit margins. It s really as simple as that.

CHAPTER 6

How To Successfully Market And Sell

How To Successfully Market And Sell

There is so much hidden potential in eBay s classified ads section. In a few moments you will discover how powerful it really is!

Let me start by explaining what a classified ad is and how to use it.

Fig. 9

What is an eBay classified Ad?
An eBay classified ad (at the time of writing) is a free advert for businesses to promote services that they may have to offer.

How To Successfully Market And Sell

How can it be used?
If for example you are an electrician, a piano or guitar teacher you could promote your services to a vast audience for free.

To place a classified ad, go to the eBay home page and select the sell link. At the bottom of the page you'll see the Advertise your business or service link.

Simply click on that and follow the steps, which will guide you through the process.

List your item for sale
Enter 3-5 words about your item. For example: Nine West women's shoes

○ Quick Sell (not suitable for vehicles)
List your item quickly using the most popular options

◉ Advanced Sell (Sell Your Item Form)
Access to all the options (reserve price, subtitle, bold and more)

Start selling

Browse categories | Recently used categories

Sell a car or motorbike | Advertise your business or service

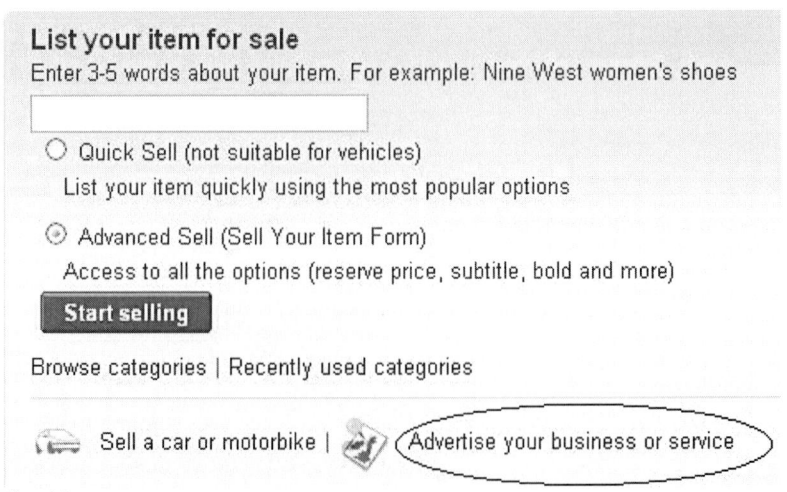

Fig. 10

How To Successfully Market And Sell

Now that s all good and well but how can we improve our chances to make money through this strategy?

How To Make Money On eBay

Let me share with you a powerful but not well known tip. It s the eBay suggestions, which comes up every time you type within the search field on the home page. You can use the eBay suggestions to type in a word that either describes what you do or describes your niche product area. For example hairdresser, plumber, mechanic or kites, kitchen mops or printer paper.

Let s use a plumber as an example. If you start typing the word plumb for example eBay s suggestion tool will provide you with search word suggestions based on what listings and searches it had and currently has.

```
plumb|
    plumbing
    plumbing tools
    plumbing fittings
    plumber
    plumbers tools
    plumbing materials
    plumbing books
            Hide eBay suggestions
```

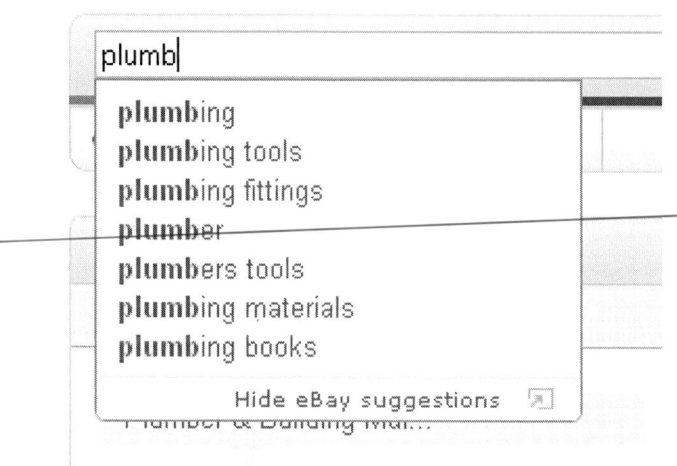

Fig. 11

How To Successfully Market And Sell

Taking the plumb example we will notice that there is a supply of and a demand for a number of things, namely;

plumbing tools, plumbing fittings, plumbers, plumber tools, plumbing materials and plumbing books.

What does this mean?
This means that there are many avenues for you as a plumber to take advantage of:

1. If you can source plumbing tools cheaply you will have a good market place on eBay.

2. If you can source plumbing materials, tools and books cheaply you will also have a good market place for them on eBay.

3. If you are a plumber the chances are individuals are seeking your services.

So as you can see you can be kept very busy working in an area that you re already familiar with.

Staying with the same concept let s look at the electrician s example.

Fig. 12 below shows the eBay suggestions when we type electricians

How To Successfully Market And Sell

```
electricians
  electricians tools
  electricians
  electricians tool kit
  electricians screwdrivers
  electricians guide
  electricians knife
  electricians bs7671
         Hide eBay suggestions
```

Fig. 12

Once again we have numerous opportunities here to make money on eBay if you are an electrician. We can once again source tool kits and screwdrivers cheaply and sell them on eBay. We can also produce an electrician's safety in the home guide, for example and also sell that on eBay.

You can also use your classified ad to promote the things that you are trying to sell. For example you could put in the ad, "if you are looking for electrician's screwdrivers then please visit my eBay listings for more details" &

So there you have it, how to make good use of eBay's classified ads to give you a nice piece of the eBay pie.

CHAPTER 7

How To Make Money Without Selling Anything

How To Make Money Without Selling Anything

Earning Through The eBay Affiliate Program

If you would like to earn money as an affiliate through a well known affiliate program, then the eBay affiliate program is an ideal opportunity for you.

What is an affiliate program?

An affiliate program is where a business rewards its affiliates for each new customer brought about by the affiliates marketing efforts. An affiliate is an individual registered to receive such rewards. This reward, in the case of the eBay affiliate program is cash.

Before you apply to do list

There are a few things that you should do before applying for the eBay affiliate program, these are namely;

1. Decide on your niche category or service you'll like to focus on, for example; Electronic components.
2. Decide on a business name to use, for example; Joe's Electronic Components.

How To Make Money Without Selling Anything

3. Decide on a business description (no more than 1000 words), for example At Joes Electronics we focus on promoting the sale of electronic components for computers to UK customers.
4. Choose a primary business model from one of the following; Shopping Comparison, Content / Website, Social Networking / Forum, Loyalty / Incentive Coupons Site, Merchant / Seller, Downloadable Software, Electronic Communications (email/IM), Other.
5. Set up a website or blog site. (Go to my blog http://ebayforprofit.blogspot.com to get help and tips with setting up a website or a blog)
6. Open a PayPal account (to open a PayPal account visit http://www.paypal.com) or have your bank account details ready for your commission payments. Once you have done all of the above you ll be ready to apply to the eBay affiliate program.

How To Make Money Without Selling Anything

How to apply for the eBay affiliate program?

Go to the eBay home page http://www.ebay.co.uk scroll down to the bottom of the page and click on the affiliate s link. (As shown in Fig. 13 below)

```
Germany | Hong Kong | India | Ireland | Italy | Korea | Malaysia | Mexico |
nd | Taiwan | Thailand | Turkey | United Kingdom | United States | Vietnam
or Charity | eBay for Business | Affiliates | Media Centre | Increase Text S
ecting IP | Policies | Feedback Forum | Site Map | Help
```

You will then be presented with the join the eBay Partner Network screen. (See the diagram below). Click on the Join Now! button.

How To Make Money Without Selling Anything

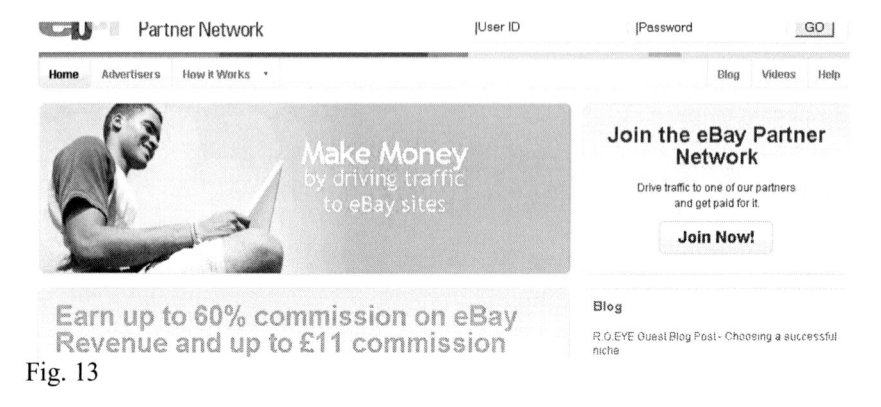

Fig. 13

Fig. 14

Be sure to tick the countries that you are interested in working in; I have chosen the UK for the purpose of this example. You may choose any or all of the nine provided.

58

How To Make Money Without Selling Anything

There is no need to tick the box for the half.com website as our focus is the eBay program. Before you can apply to the eBay affiliate program, you must read and accept the associated Terms and Conditions. Once you've done that click the continue button.

The next step involves completing some personal details, such as; your email address, name, telephone number and choosing a password. After this you'll be asked to chose a few security questions (to give your account extra protection, particularly useful if you forget your log in details).

> Join the eBay Partner Network! (Step 2 of 3)
>
> **Already an eBay AdCommerce user?**
>
> If you are currently an eBay AdCommerce user, please enter your login details.
>
> Email address
>
> [Import]
>
> **Contact Information**
>
> Email address *
>
> Confirm email address *

Fig. 15

How To Make Money Without Selling Anything

Next enter your choice of company name and business description, (these are the details that you made a note of before applying to the eBay affiliate program)

Enter your address details and choose a business type, this would be individual, company, partnership or other, (choose the one that best describes your situation)

Next enter your full website url, for example http://www.yourwebsitename.com and click the continue button.

How To Make Money Without Selling Anything

Fig. 16

After that you'll reach the final part of the application where you'll need to select how you'll like to receive your affiliate payments. You can choose PayPal (providing you have a PayPal account) or you can choose Direct Deposit to use your bank account details. (See Fig. 17 below)

How To Make Money Without Selling Anything

```
┌─────────────────────────────────────────────────────────────┐
│ Account Information                                         │
│                                                             │
│ Account Type          ⦿ Direct Deposit   ○ PayPal           │
│                       Your bank account must be located in  │
│                       the same country you                  │
│                       not be able to process your payments. │
│ Account Holder *      [                                  ]  │
│ Bank Name *           [                                  ]  │
│ Bank Sort Code *      [                        ] (?)        │
│ Account Number *      [                        ] (?)        │
│ Confirm Account Number * [                     ]            │
│                                                             │
│ Word Verification                                           │
│                                                             │
│ Please type the characters you see in the picture below     │
└─────────────────────────────────────────────────────────────┘
```
Fig. 17

After you ve completed all the required fields enter the word verification and click the submit application button. The eBay Partner Network team will be in touch with you by email, to confirm your application (usually within a week or so), be sure to check your junk mail box in case their email has gone there by mistake.

How To Make Money Without Selling Anything

Once you re registered as an affiliate you can start earning money by driving website traffic to eBay sites.

Ebay partner network tools

There are a number of useful tools provided by the eBay Partner Network, for example you can use the Creatives Generator . Creatives are colourful graphic and interactive ads which can be used to enhance your site and attract visitors to eBay pages from your website. (See Fig. 18 below)

Fig. 18

How To Make Money Without Selling Anything

Another useful tool provided by the eBay Partner Network is the Link Generator tool. The link generator allows you to create a trackable link to any of eBay Partner Network s program pages. Links are good for anyone who wants to put hyperlinks to eBay listings, search results pages, or the homepage into their site content or application.

The last tool provided by the eBay Partner Network is the Editor Kit . The Editor Kit can be used to add relevant, real-time eBay listings to your website or blog in just seconds. You can filter your results by category, keywords, or other eBay search criteria. The Editor Kit can fit into standard sized spaces like a normal ad, but it can also be sized to take up most or all of a page and used as a bare-bones shopping area. In that situation, site visitors can get an overview of the item in the ad before clicking through to eBay for more details, to bid, or to buy. (See Fig. 19 below)

How To Make Money Without Selling Anything

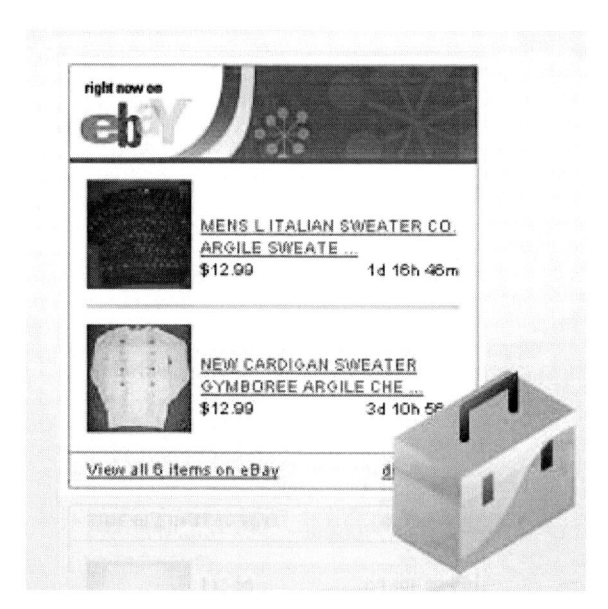

Fig. 19

For more details on the eBay Partner Network program go to https://publisher.ebaypartnernetwork.com/files/hub/en-US/tools.html

See the chapter How To Get All The Customers You Need With Web Traffic Secrets to discover more ways to generate website traffic to your eBay affiliate site or blog.

CHAPTER 8

How To Unleash The Ebay Money Making Machine

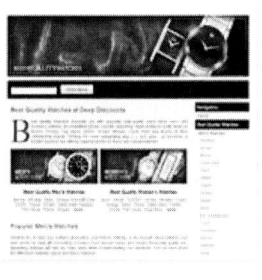

How To Unleash The Ebay Money Making Machine

If you are interested in selling eBay products, without having the hassle of stocking, despatching and tracking them, then there is an alternative solution for you. This money making endeavour is not entirely free so you can use some of your profits made from your Home Clearout Sale to re-invest into this endeavour.

Introducing the Build a Niche Store (BANS)

Build A Niche Store (BANS) is a store / website development platform which enables you to create content based websites that generate income through the eBay affiliate program. (For more about affiliate programs see the chapter on How To Make Money Without Selling Anything)

BANS Vs Drop-shipping

BANS is different from drop-shipping because of the following; with drop-shipping you are responsible for taking your customers orders and communicating with them until

How To Unleash The Ebay Money Making Machine

that order is paid for (with your customers money), the customer and order details are passed to your drop-shipper, who will then take care of your customer and their order. BANS on the other hand simply involves a potential customer clicking on a link from your electronic niche store which will refer them to an eBay listing, the order and customer involvement are taking care of by the owner of the product listing.

What are the BANS principles?

BANS works on the following 3 principles: Research, development and marketing. You research a market, develop a site of value and finally you market that site over a period of time to a niche target segment.

The "BANS process" is defined in the flow diagram below:

How To Unleash The Ebay Money Making Machine

Online Shoppers → Your Niche Store → eBay Marketplace → Affiliate Commissions

Fig. 20

Explanation: You develop your new site to target a particular niche market. Using marketing strategies you "connect" with your target market who visit your site and through the products and content it contains are directed onto eBay via your affiliate links (An affiliate is an individual registered to receive rewards for his/her marketing efforts. These rewards can be cash or some other remuneration; in this case it s cash.)

These people then register as a new eBay member and make purchases generating commission for you.

The aim when using BANS is to connect people to relevant eBay products through your own niche store.

How To Unleash The Ebay Money Making Machine

The more relevant people you connect to relevant eBay listed products (eg golfers to golf clubs) the more eBay commissions your site will generate.

How Does BANS Work?

BANS can be described using a 5 step system as described below:

Step 1: Choose A Country.

11 eBay marketplaces results in 11 different opportunities and before installing BANS your first decision is to choose which market you want to operate in.

For example, if you choose the UK you will be marketing eBay.co.uk listed products to UK internet users and if you choose Australia you will be marketing eBay.com.au listed products to Australian internet users.

How To Unleash The Ebay Money Making Machine

The 11 currently supported marketplaces are: Australia, Belgium, Canada, France, India, Italy, Netherlands, Singapore, Spain, United Kingdom and the United States.

Step 2 Choose A Niche.

This is where it gets interesting because eBay's product inventory is so wide. Taking eBay.com as an example, at any one time there are over 20 million products listed for sale across close to 30,000 categories (niches).

This provides a huge variety of options and opportunities and there are many different effective methods that can be used for determining which niche to target.

For example, you can follow and aim to capitalise on market trends, you can build a site around something that you have a genuine interest in (and hence easily add relevant and interesting content), you can base your decision on niche and

How To Unleash The Ebay Money Making Machine

keyword research and target under competitive markets (a narrow site) or alternatively you can opt for a much wider (and by definition competitive) niche with the aim of developing a fully fledged resource site and coming out on top of the market as an "authority".

For example you could create a narrow niche site focused on internet marketing and have links to eBay listings on; marketing books, marketing DVDs, marketing audios, marketing tapes and marketing videos.

The BANS community forum has a section especially set up for discussion about "choosing a niche" which covers many of these ideas and more.

Step 3 Build Your Basic Site. Once you've decided on your niche you can then build your basic site from inside the setup area of your BANS admin panel.

How To Unleash The Ebay Money Making Machine

BANS utilises the eBay category structure mentioned above along with a host of other features to enable you to pinpoint those products you want to display inside the store part of your site.

Select a template, upload a logo and you have the foundation of your new site built.

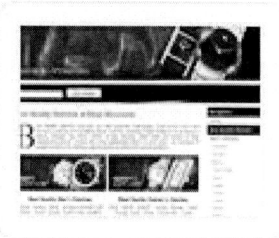

Step 4 Develop Your Site.

Depending how wide your target niche is and how deep you're planning on going into it there is an almost endless variety of ways in which you can develop your site to make it valuable" for its target market and hence a better earner in the eBay affiliate program.

Template customisations, store page creation and content development are standard with some BANS users going

How To Unleash The Ebay Money Making Machine

deeper and deeper adding things like videos, Blogs, directories and forums.

Again, sections in the BANS community forum are set up to enable the discussion of such ideas and strategies to evolve.

Step 5 Marketing.
There are many different ways of connecting your site to your target market and these can loosely be defined as marketing.

The most common include SEM (search engine marketing), (SEM is a form of Internet marketing that seeks to promote websites by increasing their visibility in search engine result pages). SEM comprises of SEO (search engine optimization). (SEO is the process of improving the volume or quality of traffic to a web site from search engines), and PPC (Pay Per Click advertising - PPC is an Internet advertising model used on search engines, advertising networks, and content sites, such as blogs, in which advertisers pay their host only when their ad is clicked.), article marketing, (Article marketing is a

How To Unleash The Ebay Money Making Machine

type of advertising in which businesses write short articles related to their respective industry. These articles are made available for distribution and publication in the marketplace. Each article contains a bio box and byline that include references and contact information for the author's business. Well-written content articles released for free distribution have the potential of increasing the authors business credibility within their market as well as attracting new clients.)   free-ads advertising, viral techniques like video, and the direct purchase of advertising on related sites.

By following these 5 principles and going as deep into your target niche as required, your new site will begin to generate eBay affiliate commissions. You can then take what you've learnt and repeat the process in as many niche markets as you want to operate in.

(Source Build a Niche Store)

For more details on the Build a Niche Store and links visit my blog at http://ebayforprofit.blogspot.com

CHAPTER 9

How To Make Money In Auto-pilot

How To Make Money In Auto-pilot

In this chapter you will learn how an auto-responder will help you to sell your own products, other people s products, or anything else.

What is an Auto-responder?

Typically, an auto-responder is a computer program that automatically sends e-mails to its subscribers. They can be very simple or quite complex. The owner of the auto-responder will write several email messages in advance then schedule the messages to be sent at pre-defined intervals. Subscribers will sign up to receive the emails.

Where Will My Subscribers Come From?

The auto-responder program will allow you to create a small form which you can insert on your niche store website so that visitors to your site can subscribe by entering their name and email address.

10 ways to increase your revenue

The following are 10 ways that you can use an auto-responder to advertise and thus increase your revenue. (Go to my blog http://ebayforprofit.blogspot.com to

How To Make Money In Auto-pilot

get more details on auto-responders, how to use them and where to find them)

Here we go:

Way No. 1: Publish a newsletter for your opt-in subscribers. Your auto-responder can submit your newsletter on a schedule you pre-determine, for example daily, weekly, monthly, quarterly or whatever suits you. Your newsletter can keep your visitors informed about your services and/or products, while building your reputation as an expert in your niche or field.

Way No. 2: Publish a newsletter only for your affiliates. Announce when you are having a sale or promotion. Offer your affiliates all of the sales materials, as well as tips and advice they can use to increase their commissions. (Go to my blog http://ebayforprofit.blogspot.com to learn more about affiliates (generally speaking affiliates are individuals that will help with the promotion of your products and services for a percentage of the sale)

Way No. 3: Write reviews of current books, software, other products, music, e-books, videos, etc., and put each review in an auto-responder with an affiliate link to that product. When your subscribers make a purchase through your affiliate link you ll receive a commission for the sale. (Go to my blog http://ebayforprofit.blogspot.com to get a list of some companies offering affiliate programs that you can join)

Way No. 4: Create articles to distribute through your auto responder. Writing and distributing articles that provide relevant and good information is a powerful tool to build your business credibility. Articles are not sales copy. Provide helpful information only and include a bio or a resource box at the end of your article. The resource box should include your name and what services, products you provide and could include a link to your website or blog.

How To Make Money In Auto-pilot

See the example in Fig. 20 below taking from http://KensAdvertisingAndMarketingArticles.blogspot.com/

Ken Ajoku is the CEO of The Kajoku Group, a company dedicated to creating and maintaining a number of businesses. These businesses include; Property, Publishing, Business Consulting and a number of online business ventures. Go to The Kajoku Group blog for more details.

Fig. 20

As you can see from the example Ken has provided his name and company details at the bottom of his free advertising article blog. (This is commonly known as the resource box or bio) You can follow the same example, by the way Ken s company published this very book you are reading (Bless you Ken and many thanks to the Kajoku Group).

Use your auto responder to inform subscribers of new articles you post to your blog or website. You can also offer to allow your users to publish your articles on their own websites but only if they agree to not make any changes and to include your resource box or bio intact. (This is a good way of generating more traffic to your blog or website)

How To Make Money In Auto-pilot

Way No. 5: Automate your sales process. When writing ads, include a way to link to your auto responder to capture the email address of your potential customer. You can do this by offering your potential customer something for free. See the Fig. 21 below.

Fig. 21

In Fig. 21 above you ll notice that a FREE 6-Day Business Start up Course is on offer in exchange for a name and email address. Potential customers will be more than happy to provide their details because it s worth the exchange. The key to success using this method is to ensure that you include a privacy statement at the bottom; this gives the user more confidence to provide you with their details.

How To Make Money In Auto-pilot

Way No. 6: Distribute advertising to your subscribers using your auto-responder. You can create a picture ad similar to the one shown in Fig. 22 below to advertise your products.

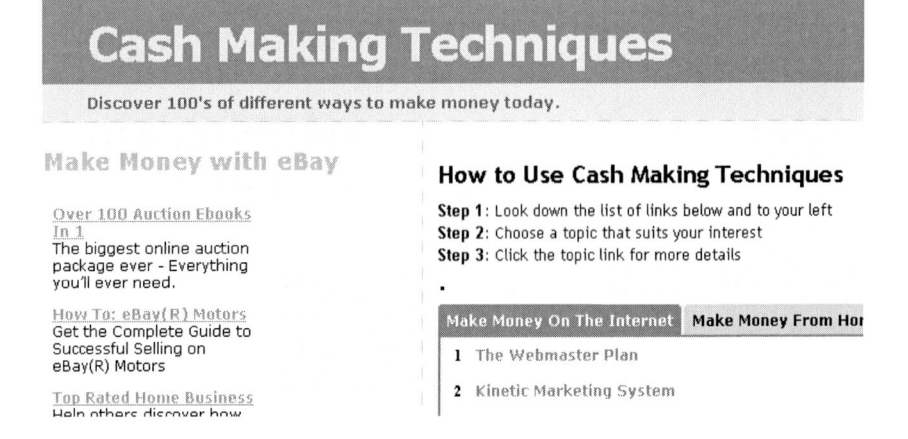

Cash Making Techniques

Discover 100's of different ways to make money today.

Make Money with eBay

<u>Over 100 Auction Ebooks In 1</u>
The biggest online auction package ever - Everything you'll ever need.

<u>How To: eBay(R) Motors</u>
Get the Complete Guide to Successful Selling on eBay(R) Motors

<u>Top Rated Home Business</u>
Help others discover how

How to Use Cash Making Techniques

Step 1: Look down the list of links below and to your left
Step 2: Choose a topic that suits your interest
Step 3: Click the topic link for more details

Make Money On The Internet	Make Money From Hor
1 The Webmaster Plan	
2 Kinetic Marketing System	

Fig. 22

Way No. 7: Distribute an email course. Each day have your auto-responder send out another lesson. Just be sure that each lesson has quality content, and is not a sales pitch. (As shown in way 5), when the course ends continue to auto respond them by sending them related promotional material.

How To Make Money In Auto-pilot

Way No. 8: Use your auto-responder to send a reminder about your service or product after a visitor has completed your course for example. This will increase the possibility of sales from visitors who have taken your course but are dragging their feet about actually making a purchase decision.

Way No. 9: Distribute free reports. This gives your visitor an idea of the type of information you provide and the quality of your product or scrvice.

Way No. 10: Use an auto-responder on your order page. Post a request form for visitors to be notified of special offers or discounts in the future. This creates a very effective mailing list that contains the names of people who are already your customers.

These are just a few ideas of how to utilize your auto-responders. Your sales revenue can increase dramatically if you start using auto-responders to advertise your products

How To Make Money In Auto-pilot

and services. And it doesn t cost a penny you can find many auto-responders for free on the Web (for example, http://www.responders.com and http://www.freeautobot.com can be downloaded and used for free, there are also more sophisticated ones that I personally recommend - more details at http://ebayforprofit.blogspot.com).

I do sincerely hope that this tip will help you to maximise your eBay sales revenues and that you ve increased your earnings by following the guidelines that we ve discussed in the previous chapters.

CHAPTER 10

How To Get All The Customers You Need With Web Traffic Secrets

How To Get All The Customers You Need

Is there any point having a website selling stuff if nobody knows that it s there?

Yes - you re right. Absolutely no point at all!

The funny thing is that I have spoken to numerous people who believe that all one has to do is to create a nice looking website, and as if by magic you ll have all the visitors you want looking at it.

Not so I m afraid.

In this chapter I ll share with you web traffic pulling tips that you can use to drive large numbers of targeted traffic to your eBay listings, niche store and your eBay classified ads.
Are you ready?
Ok, let s get going &

4 Web traffic pulling strategies

How To Get All The Customers You Need

I m going to briefly address 4 strategies, which are namely; (1) Classified Ad Submitting, (2) Web Directory Listing, (3) Article submission, and (4) Forum posting.

Let s take a look at the first web traffic pulling strategy
(1) Classified Ads Submitting.
We covered what a classified ad is in the How To Successfully Market And Sell chapter.

To fully maximise this strategy you will need to post your services and or products in as many classified ads websites as possible. You can get a list of free sites to post your ads in by typing Free classified x ads , or post x free classified ads , or or free x classified ads UK into a search engine of your choice. (Replacing the x for your product or service niche area - for example; Free classified laptop computer ads)

Be sure to read each site s terms and conditions for ad posting so that you do not violate them. Also while visiting websites have a look at other peoples postings to give you a

How To Get All The Customers You Need

general idea of the ad format.

Your objective here is to get as much targeted visitors to view your product listings as possible. The more the specific your postings the better the quality of your visitors and the more likely that more of your visitors will become customers. You can find more details and links to helpful websites, both paid for and free at my blog site
go to http://ebayforprofit.blogspot.com

(2) Web directory

A web directory is similar to a yellow pages directory except it s on the web, businesses and individuals will list their website details in a section as close to their industry sector as possible within that web directory. You can get a list of these by using the a search engine of your choice and typing Free Directory Listing or Free Business Directory or Add a free link . When posting to directories you should follow their instructions carefully to get the full benefit of the service. This type of posting is quite simple to do and is very effective for pulling in web traffic.

How To Get All The Customers You Need

For details and links, go to my blog

http://ebayforprofit.blogspot.com

(3) Article submission
Article submission requires a little bit more thought and time and is normally done by copywriters. So if you don t consider yourself an author then you may wish to consider outsourcing the writing task. New articles are highly sought after by article websites and search engines.

So if you can write fresh content you re onto a winning traffic pulling formula. To get a targeted list of article websites to submit your articles to type into your preferred search engine, free x article submission , or, free x article submission sites , or, directory of free article submission . (Replacing the x for your product or service niche area)

More details and links to both paid for and free services can be found at my blog

 http://ebayforprofit.blogspot.com

How To Get All The Customers You Need

(4) Forum Posting

Forum posting as its name suggest involves making posts on forum websites.

First of all you will need to find forums that match your niche area, you can do this by typing into your favourite search engine, x discussion forums , or, x forums , or, x UK forums , or, x message forums , and free x forums , (Replacing the x with your product / niche area of interest or expertise).

Once you have found suitable websites you will need to make appropriate posts. Avoid signing up to use a forum only to post an advert. Your post may be deemed as Spam and most probably deleted; in some cases they will also ban you from further posts. The key is to make genuine posts. You help others and at the same time help yourself. Let me

How To Get All The Customers You Need

give you an example. Let s say someone put up a forum post Does anyone know how to fix a broken computer?

Now it just so happens that you are an expert in this field. You would register as a user in that particular forum and give suggestions to the problem at hand. But what good is this you may ask yourself?

Well this is a fantastic opportunity for you to promote your services not only to that user with the problem but also to any other user who may come across a similar problem. What you could do is add a bio or resource box within your administration area of your user account. (We covered bio and resource boxes in the How To Make Money In Auto-pilot chapter) The bio could say Jonathan Smith is the Managing Director of www.HearingEquipmentForYou.com

How To Get All The Customers You Need

a company that has been featured on eBay since May 2002, the company specialises in selling equipment for individuals who suffer from hearing disabilities. Visit their website now to claim your free hearing test voucher or email the team at help@HearingEquipmentForYou.com for further information.

So there you have it 4 powerful web pulling techniques that you can implement today to bring you tons of website traffic!

Go to http://ebayforprofit.blogspot.com
For more links, tips and short cuts to your website traffic success!

These techniques are very effective ways of maximising your eBay profits. I hope that by now you are more familiar with

How To Get All The Customers You Need

eBay and have learned how to turn the eBay platform into a money-spinning machine.

I wish you all the very best in your money making endeavours, and I hope that you re able to make as much money as any expert eBay seller makes today, and even more.

I ll love to hear your success stories, comments, suggestions, feedback and aspirations, please go to my blog http://ebayforprofit.blogspot.com and leave
your comments there. I value your feedback and I m always trying to improve my products and services available to you.

Good luck!

BONUS CHAPTER
How To Make Money Blogging

How To Make Money Blogging

I ve added this chapter as a bonus chapter to give you another money-spinning tip, it s not necessarily an eBay money making technique but worth a mention nevertheless.

Blogging is a technique that requires no previous technical experience at all. If you are not using this strategy, or are not aware of it, the chances are you may be losing thousands of pounds worth of extra income.

In a nutshell, a blog is a website on which an individual writes journal-type entries about a subject matter of their choice. Blogs can be about anything from current events in the media to an individual s personal life. The term blog is short for weblog.

To make money from a blog you need to create a blog site and monetise it. Every time a reader clicks on one of your ads you get paid. This is another way of making money without spending any money.

How To Make Money Blogging

Here s the theory, a user will read the article because he or she is interested in the topic. Once they have finished reading they will want to take action of some kind, depending on the article. They will then read the ads to see if there is anything of interest there. If there is something of interest there then they will be compelled to click on the ad to find out more.

Every time that user clicks on any of the Ads by Google ads then you the site owner will be credited. These credits can range from pennies to pounds per click the amounts will depend on the popularity of the keywords in your blog posts.

Go to https://adwords.google.com/select/KeywordTool to get a rough idea of which keywords are more popular than others. Simply type in a keyword and select the get keyword ideas. Please note you will be prompted either to log in with your Google account or to create a new account before you ll be able to use the free service, it s a very useful tool so I would recommend that you create a free account with Google.

How To Make Money Blogging

What are 'Ads by Google'?

Ads by Google are ads generated by Google s Adsense program. Google AdSense is a program that can give you advertising revenue from each page on your website. AdSense delivers relevant text and image ads that are precisely targeted to your site and your site content. (Source: http://www.google.com/services/adsense_tour/index.html)

How to Create a Blog Site
Let me show you step by step how you can create a blog site and be up and running within a few minutes.

Step 1 Create an Account
Blogger and WordPress are two examples of the numerous blog providers you can use to create your blog account. We will use Blogger to illustrate how to set up a blog account.

To get started with Blogger, you ll need to create your free account. On the Blogger homepage, www.blogger.com click the "Create Your Blog Now" button: (See Fig. 23)

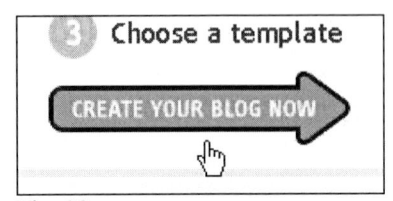

Fig. 23
Screenshot: Create A New Blog
(Courtesy of Blogger help)

Next you'll be prompted to create a Google Account. If you already have a Google Account you will need to sign in first. After you've done that, you'll need to enter a display name (this is the name used to sign your blog posts), and accept Blogger's Terms of Service.

Once you're done with this, you'll be prompted to create a Blog and get started!

Step 2 Name Your Blog
Once you ve created an account you ll need to name your blog. Choose a suitable blog title and blog address, once you have done this click the continue button. (See Fig. 24 & 25)

How To Make Money Blogging

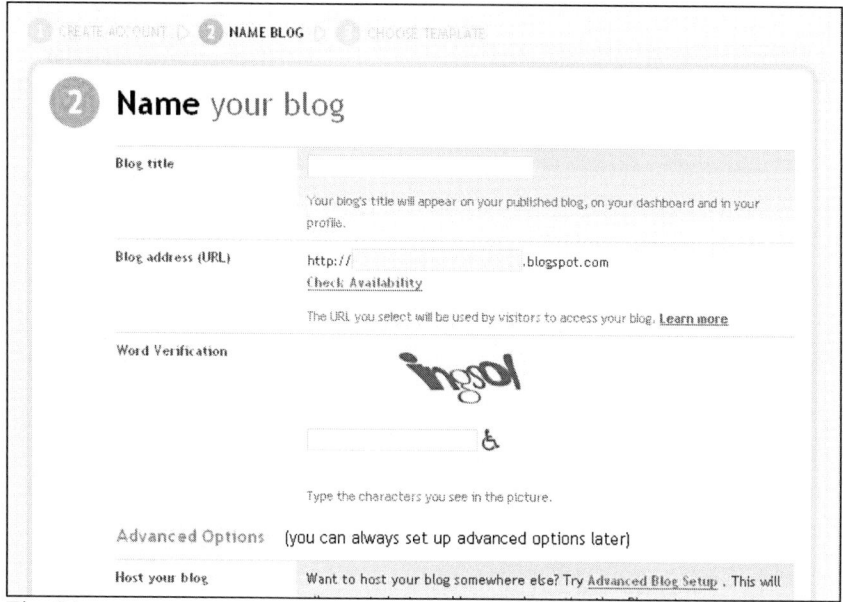

Fig. 24

Fig. 25

Step 3 Choose a Template

How To Make Money Blogging

Choose a template that you like the look of and select continue. (See Fig. 26 below)

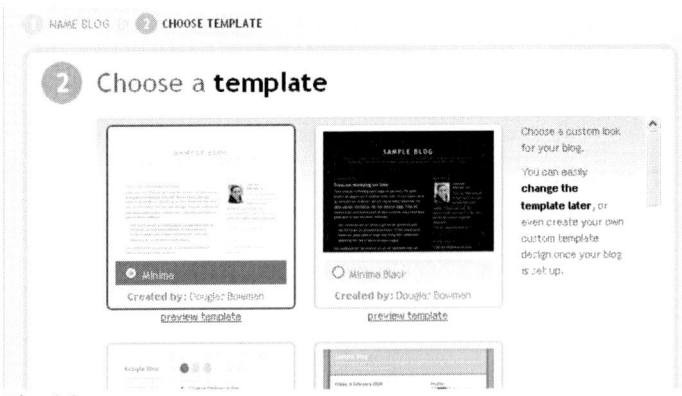

Fig. 26

You will see the following message. You are now ready to start blogging. (See Fig. 27 below)

Fig. 27

Step 4 Post Your First Blog Post

How To Make Money Blogging

Start by giving your post a title (optional), then enter the post itself:

When you're done, click the Preview link to make sure it's ready to go:

Once you're satisfied with your post, click the **Publish** button. This will publish your new post.

Step 5 Monetise Your Blog

Once you have made a few posts then you will be ready to add Google Adsense to your blog to monetise it.

Fig. 28

Select the monetise tab. (See fig. 29 below)

How To Make Money Blogging

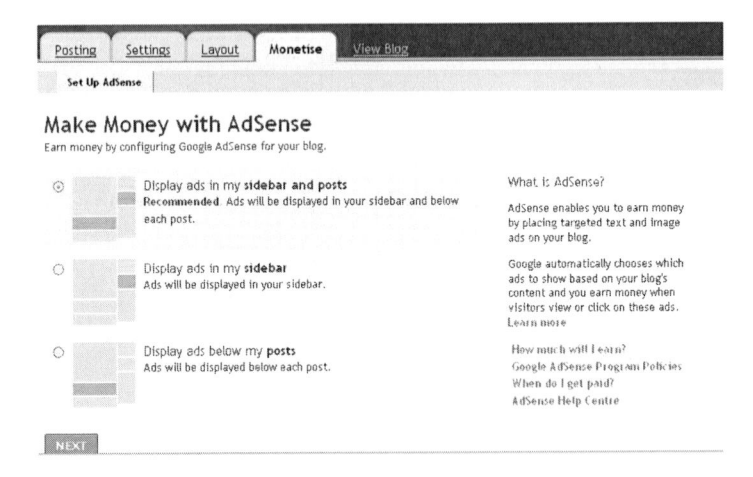

Fig. 29

How To Make Money Blogging

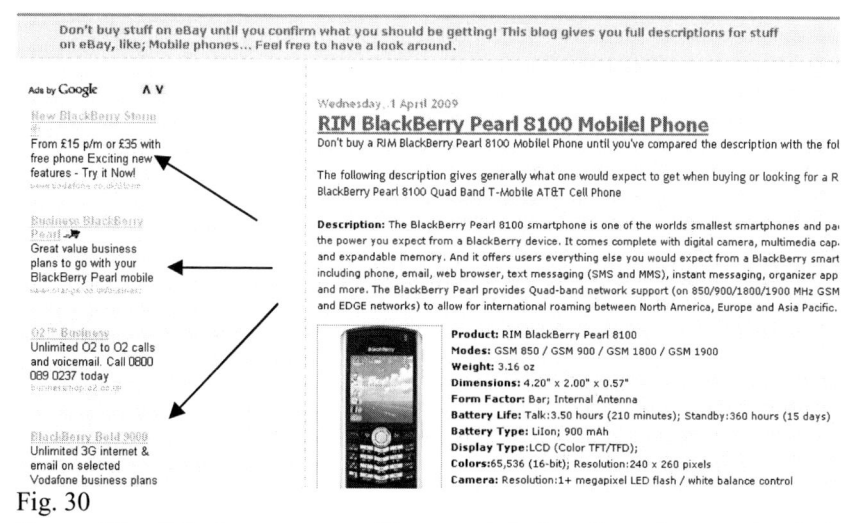

Fig. 30

From Fig. 30 above you will see Ads by Google on the left hand side. Every time a user clicks on any of these ads displayed the site owner receives money from Google.

You don t have to limit yourself to eBay related topics, you can blog about absolutely anything; your hobbies, your experience, your business, even your life story.

Here s a blog for example, (see Fig. 31) about marketing articles
(screen shot taken from:
 KensAdvertisingAndMarketingArticles.blogspot.com)
once again you can see how the Google Ads are displayed on the left hand side of the screen.

How To Make Money Blogging

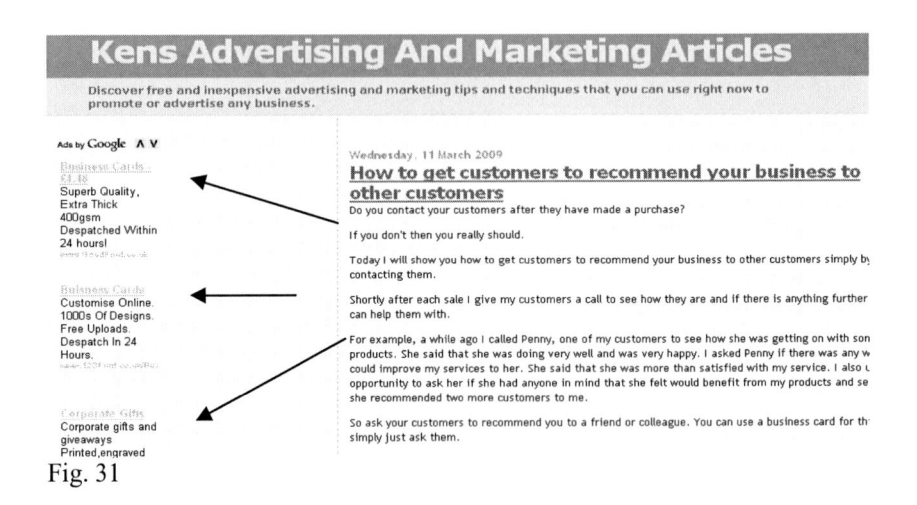

Fig. 31

You may have heard stories about people earning money from Google Adsense and must have also heard from skeptical people who may believe that it is a myth, let me assure you that making money from Adsense is not a myth at all. In fact, it is a very intelligent way of earning money via sites like Blogger.com without spending any money at all.

The whole concept of Adsense works on the principle of relevant keyword content. The more on topic and relevant your content the more targeted your Adsense ads will be, as I ve shown you in the previous examples.

How To Make Money Blogging

As an Adsense publisher you will have to stick to the terms and conditions, so I suggest you read them carefully as misuse of the account can cause it to be either suspended or closed, Google doesn t take lightly to misuse.

The example blog I mentioned previously KensAdvertisingAndMarketingArticles.blogspot.com , (Fig. 31) gives its readers free advertising and marketing articles while displaying Google Ads on the left-hand side.

I believe that everyone and anyone can write. So why not write and get paid for it? Why not spend a little time (and no money) to take advantage of Google s Adsense and make money online by working from the comfort of your home. The demand for Adsense as an advertising medium has brought with it the need to build sites with fresh and quality content. So if your website can have a steady supply of articles with the proper keywords that relate to their site contents, it will attract hundreds or maybe thousands of visitors. And when your site gets thousands of visitor clicks,

How To Make Money Blogging

your site page automatically starts showing higher up in the search engine results.

At the following link http://adwords.google.com/support you can discover all the benefits of using Google Adwords and how to get started, read success stories, learn from others through seminars and make use of the Adwords help forum.

To summarise here are the 4 steps to follow using this strategy.

(i)   Create your blog

(ii)   Populate the blog with original content (avoid copying stuff from other sites, as the content will not register as original content in the search engines) Google s search engine is hungry for original content and will give priority to sites with original content.

(iii)   Monetise your blog by adding Google Adsense.

    Write consistently, try and make a habit of adding new content as often as you can. (The more the better.)

How To Make Money Blogging

I trust that you ve enjoyed reading this book. I welcome you to add any comments or feed back you have at my blog site http://ebayforprofit.blogspot.com

I d love to hear how you found the book or better still your success stories after you have implemented some or all of the strategies that I ve shared with you.

Kind regards and all the best.

Dan Gibson

My Make Money on eBay Notes

My Make Money on eBay Notes

My Make Money on eBay Notes

My Make Money on eBay Notes

My Make Money on eBay Notes

My Make Money on eBay Notes

My Make Money on eBay Notes

My Make Money on eBay Action Plan

Make Money on eBay Action Plan

To succeed I suggest that you commit yourself to spending 1 – 1½ hours a day working on making money.

Consistency is the secret to your success!

Use the following daily schedule to help you plan which aspects you intend to work on and when you ll be committed to doing them.

For example you may want to spend one hour between 6 and 7am writing new blog entries for your newly developed blog. And you may also commit yourself to spending thirty minutes every day between 7 and 7.30am to checking eBay s latest listings in your particular niche area (so that you keep abreast of the competition and new developments for example)

Your hand entries could look something like this:

Monday

6-7am Add 3 new How I made a million pounds blog entries

7-8am Check the latest eBay listings on Canon Digital cameras.

Make Money on eBay Action Plan

Day: Monday

6-7am _____

7-8am _____

8-9am _____

9-10am _____

11-12pm _____

12-1pm _____

1-2pm _____

2-3pm _____

3-4pm _____

4-5pm _____

5-6pm _____

6-7pm _____

7-8pm _____

Make Money on eBay Action Plan

8-9pm _____

10-11pm _____

11-12pm _____

12-1am _____

1-2am _____

2-3am _____

3-4am _____

4-5am _____

5-6am _____

Day: Tuesday

6-7am _____

7-8am _____

8-9am _____

9-10am _____

Make Money on eBay Action Plan

11-12pm _____

12-1pm _____

1-2pm _____

2-3pm _____

3-4pm _____

4-5pm _____

5-6pm _____

6-7pm _____

7-8pm _____

8-9pm _____

10-11pm _____

11-12pm _____

12-1am _____

1-2am _____

2-3am _____

Make Money on eBay Action Plan

3-4am _____

4-5am _____

5-6am _____

Day: Wednesday

6-7am _____

7-8am _____

8-9am _____

9-10am _____

11-12pm _____

12-1pm _____

1-2pm _____

2-3pm _____

3-4pm _____

4-5pm _____

5-6pm _____

Make Money on eBay Action Plan

6-7pm _____

7-8pm _____

8-9pm _____

10-11pm _____

11-12pm _____

12-1am _____

1-2am _____

2-3am _____

3-4am _____

4-5am _____

5-6am _____

Day: Thursday

6-7am _____

7-8am _____

Make Money on eBay Action Plan

8-9am _____

9-10am _____

11-12pm _____

12-1pm _____

1-2pm _____

2-3pm _____

3-4pm _____

4-5pm _____

5-6pm _____

6-7pm _____

7-8pm _____

8-9pm _____

10-11pm _____

11-12pm _____

Make Money on eBay Action Plan

12-1am _____

1-2am _____

2-3am _____

3-4am _____

4-5am _____

5-6am _____

Day: Friday

6-7am _____

7-8am _____

8-9am _____

9-10am _____

11-12pm _____

12-1pm _____

1-2pm _____

Make Money on eBay Action Plan

2-3pm _____

3-4pm _____

4-5pm _____

5-6pm _____

6-7pm _____

7-8pm _____

8-9pm _____

10-11pm _____

11-12pm _____

12-1am _____

1-2am _____

2-3am _____

3-4am _____

4-5am _____

5-6am _____

Make Money on eBay Action Plan

Day: Saturday

6-7am _____

7-8am _____

8-9am _____

9-10am _____

11-12pm _____

12-1pm _____

1-2pm _____

2-3pm _____

3-4pm _____

4-5pm _____

5-6pm _____

6-7pm _____

7-8pm _____

Make Money on eBay Action Plan

8-9pm _____

10-11pm _____

11-12pm _____

12-1am _____

1-2am _____

2-3am _____

3-4am _____

4-5am _____

5-6am _____

Day: Sunday

6-7am _____

7-8am _____

8-9am _____

Make Money on eBay Action Plan

9-10am _____

11-12pm _____

12-1pm _____

1-2pm _____

2-3pm _____

3-4pm _____

4-5pm _____

5-6pm _____

6-7pm _____

7-8pm _____

8-9pm _____

10-11pm _____

11-12pm _____

12-1am _____

Make Money on eBay Action Plan

1-2am _____

2-3am _____

3-4am _____

4-5am _____

5-6am _____